A Benjamin Blog
and his Inquisitive Dog
Investigation

Exploring Rivers

Anita Ganeri

Raintree

Raintree is an imprint of Capstone Global Library Limited, a company incorporated in England and Wales having its registered office at 7 Pilgrim Street, London, EC4V 6LB – Registered company number: 6695582

www.raintreepublishers.co.uk
myorders@raintreepublishers.co.uk

Edited by Dan Nunn, Rebecca Rissman, and Helen Cox Cannons
Designed by Joanna Hinton-Malivoire
Original illustrations © Capstone Global Library Ltd
Illustrated by Sernur ISIK
Picture research by Mica Brancic
Originated by Capstone Global Library Ltd
Production by Helen McCreath
Printed and bound in China

ISBN 978 1 406 27103 4
17 16 15 14 13
10 9 8 7 6 5 4 3 2 1

British Library Cataloguing in Publication Data
A full catalogue record for this book is available from the British Library.

Acknowledgements
We would like to thank the following for permission to reproduce photographs: Corbis p. 20 (© Eric and David Hosking); eoimages p. 25 (NASA); FLPA p. 29 top (Mark Sisson); Getty Images pp. 6 (DEA/G. COZZI), 16 (Ritterbach Ritterbach), 18 (Farhana Jenny), 22 (© Peter Walton Photography); Naturepl. com p. 7 (© Jim Clare); Photoshot p. 27 (© NHPA/ Nigel Hicks); Robert Harding World Imagery p. 9 (Ben Pipe Photography/Robert Hard); Shutterstock pp. 4 (© Josef Hanus), 5 (© feiyuezhangjie), 8 (© atm2003), 10 (© Chawalit S.), 11 (© LysFoto), 14 (© Porojnicu Stelian), 17 (© David Hughes), 23 (© LehaKoK); SuperStock pp. 12 (Hemis.fr), 13 (Wolfgang Kaehler), 15 (Marka), 19 (age fotostock/ Martin Zwick), 21 (Minden Pictures/Ingo Arndt), 24 (Hemis.fr), 26 (imagebroker.net), 29 bottom (age fotostock/Martin Zwick).

Front cover of a river in the Altai Mountains, Russia, reproduced with permission of Shutterstock (© straga).

We would like to thank Michael Bright for his invaluable help in the preparation of this book.

Every effort has been made to contact copyright holders of material reproduced in this book. Any omissions will be rectified in subsequent printings if notice is given to the publisher.

Some words are shown in bold, **like this**. You can find out what they mean by looking in the glossary.

Contents

Exploring rivers!

Hello! My name's Benjamin Blog and this is Barko Polo, my **inquisitive** dog. (He's named after the ancient ace explorer **Marco Polo**.) We have just got back from our latest adventure – exploring rivers around the world. We put this book together from some of the blog posts we wrote on the way.

BARKO'S BLOG-TASTIC RIVER FACTS

Rivers flow through almost every country in the world. They sweep down from mountains and across **plains**, carrying water to the sea. This is the Yulong River in China.

Rushing river

Posted by: Ben Blog | 28 February at 9.15 a.m.

We started our trip here on Lake Victoria in East Africa. It is the main **source** of the River Nile, the world's longest river. It flows out of the lake as a stream. The source is the place where a river starts. Other rivers start off as mountain **springs** or flow from **glaciers**.

BARKO'S BLOG-TASTIC RIVER FACTS

The icy Gangotri glacier is high up in the Himalayas in India. In spring and summer, the end of the glacier melts and starts off a stream that becomes the River Ganges.

Canyon carving

At the start, a river flows fast and carries along boulders, pebbles, and sand. These grind away at the river bed, carving out valleys and **canyons**. This is the Grand Canyon in the United States. It was carved out by the Colorado River and is 446 kilometres (277 miles) long and 1½ kilometres (1 mile) deep in places.

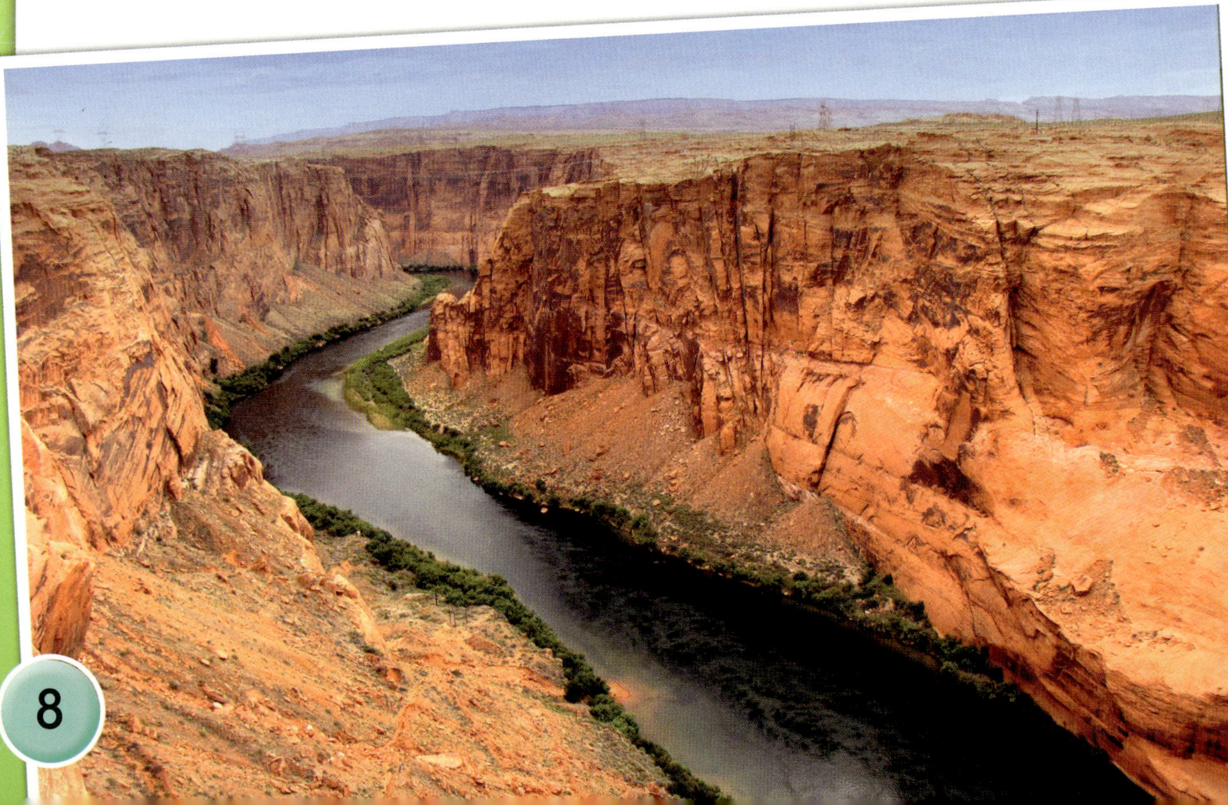

BARKO'S BLOG-TASTIC RIVER FACTS

In the mountains, rivers carve out steep-sided, V-shaped valleys, like this one in Nepal. It was made by the Dudh Kosi River that flows down Mount Everest.

Wonderful waterfalls

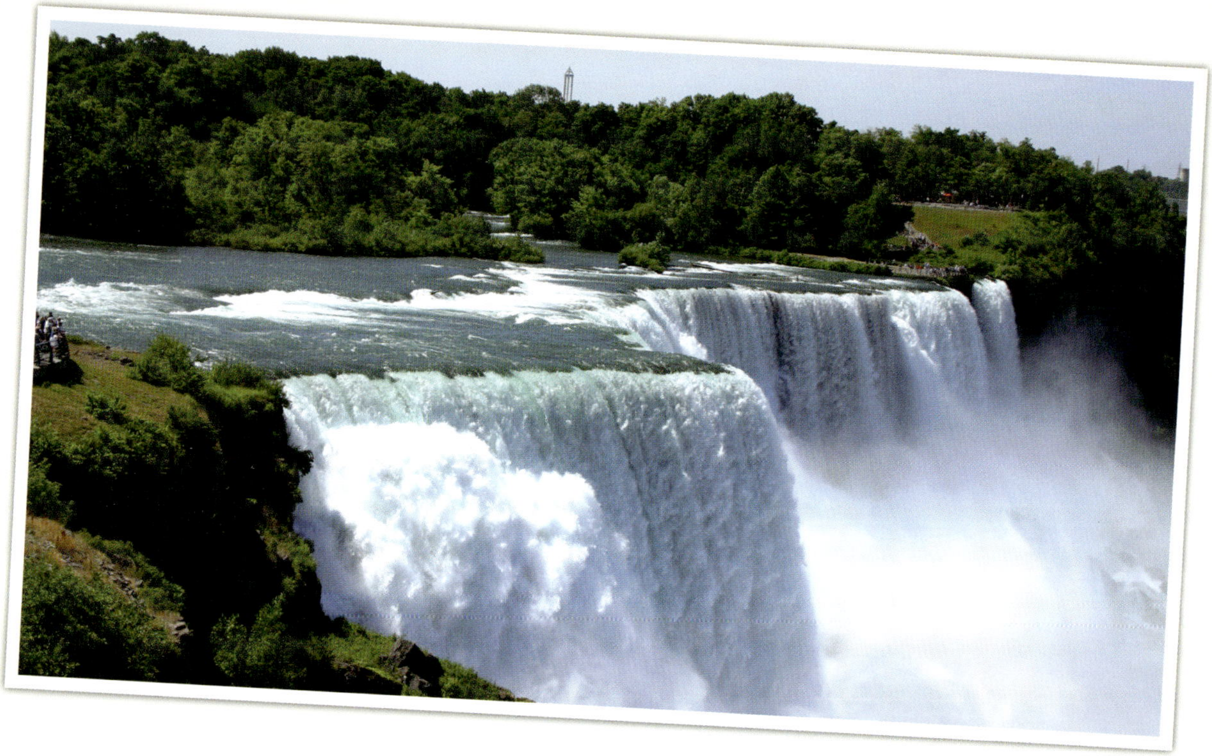

We are visiting Niagara Falls on the border between Canada and the United States. This is probably the world's most famous waterfall, so I took loads of photos. Waterfalls form when a river flows over a shelf of hard rock, eating away at the soft rock underneath.

10

BARKO'S BLOG-TASTIC RIVER FACTS

Angel Falls in Venezuela is the tallest waterfall in the world. Here, the River Churun plunges 979 metres (3,212 feet) down Devil's Mountain. What an awesome sight!

Winding rivers

Posted by: Ben Blog | 1 May at 5.11 p.m.

Our last day in the United States was spent on the mighty Mississippi River. I wanted to see its **meanders** – here is a snap I took from a helicopter. Meanders are great loops or bends made as the river swings from side to side. This happens when the river winds its way slowly across flat land.

BARKO'S BLOG-TASTIC RIVER FACTS

As a river flows along, other streams flow into it. They are called **tributaries**. Some are big enough to count as rivers in their own right. This is the Maranon River, a tributary of the Amazon River.

Running away to sea

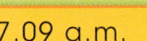   

Today we are by the Black Sea in Romania. Here, the River Danube dumps its load of rocks and sand before it flows into the sea. It forms a fan-shaped area of new land, called a **delta**. The Danube Delta is huge, and is home to some amazing animals, such as these pelicans.

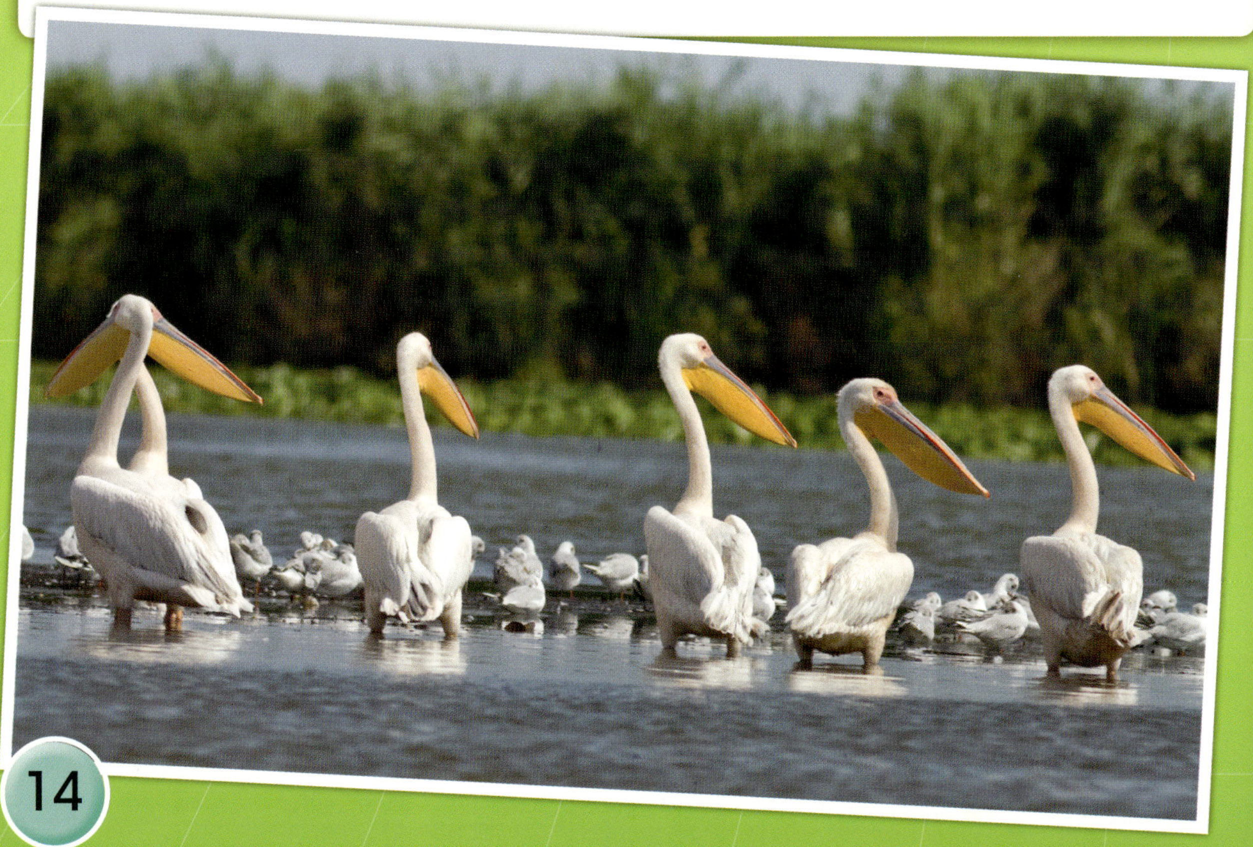

BARKO'S BLOG-TASTIC RIVER FACTS

Some rivers do not flow into the sea. The Okavango River flows into the Kalahari Desert in Botswana. In the rainy season, it's full of wildlife – like these hippopotamuses!

Riverside gardens

Posted by: Ben Blog | 26 July at 8.32 a.m.

Plenty of plants live on rivers, but these water lilies on the Amazon River are the biggest that I have ever seen. Their enormous pads float on the surface and can grow 2.5 metres (8 feet) across. They are supposed to be strong enough for humans to sit on, so I'm going to give it a try.

Posted by: Ben Blog | 26 July at 10.42 a.m.

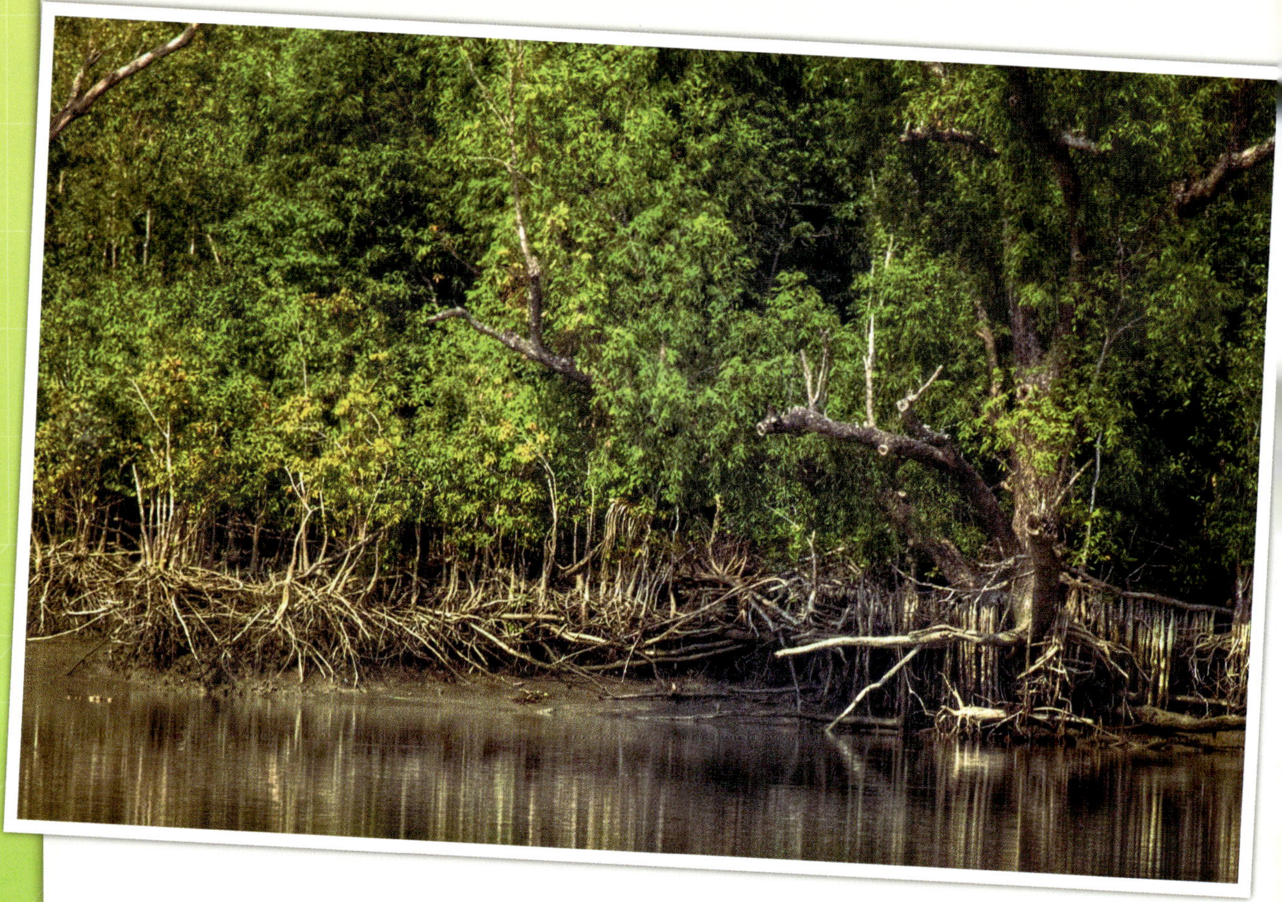

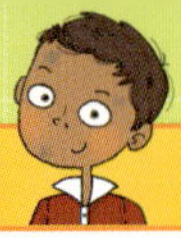

Next stop on our trip was the Sundarbans. It is a massive forest of mangrove trees that grows across the **delta** of the Ganges and Brahmaputra Rivers in India and Bangladesh. Mangroves have roots that sprout from their trunks. These fix the trees firmly in the mud.

BARKO'S BLOG-TASTIC RIVER FACTS

These river red gum trees grow along the banks of rivers in Australia. Their branches fall into the water and make useful shelters for fish. Animals also eat their fallen leaves.

Watery wildlife

Posted by: Ben Blog | 12 August at 2.22 p.m.

Rivers are home to some amazing animals. I spotted these torrent ducks on the Urubamba River, in the Andes Mountains. The fast-flowing water is dangerous, but the ducks are strong swimmers and divers. They also have claws on their feet to grip the slippery rocks.

20

BARKO'S BLOG-TASTIC RIVER FACTS

Otters have **streamlined** bodies and webbed paws for swimming after their **prey** of fish. They also have thick, waterproof fur to keep them dry and warm. Lucky otters – dogs just get wet!

Back in Australia, we went out on the river with some scientists who are studying saltwater crocodiles. These massive reptiles lie in the water, looking like logs. Then they attack fish and other animals that come to the river for a drink. I snapped this one before it tried to snap me!

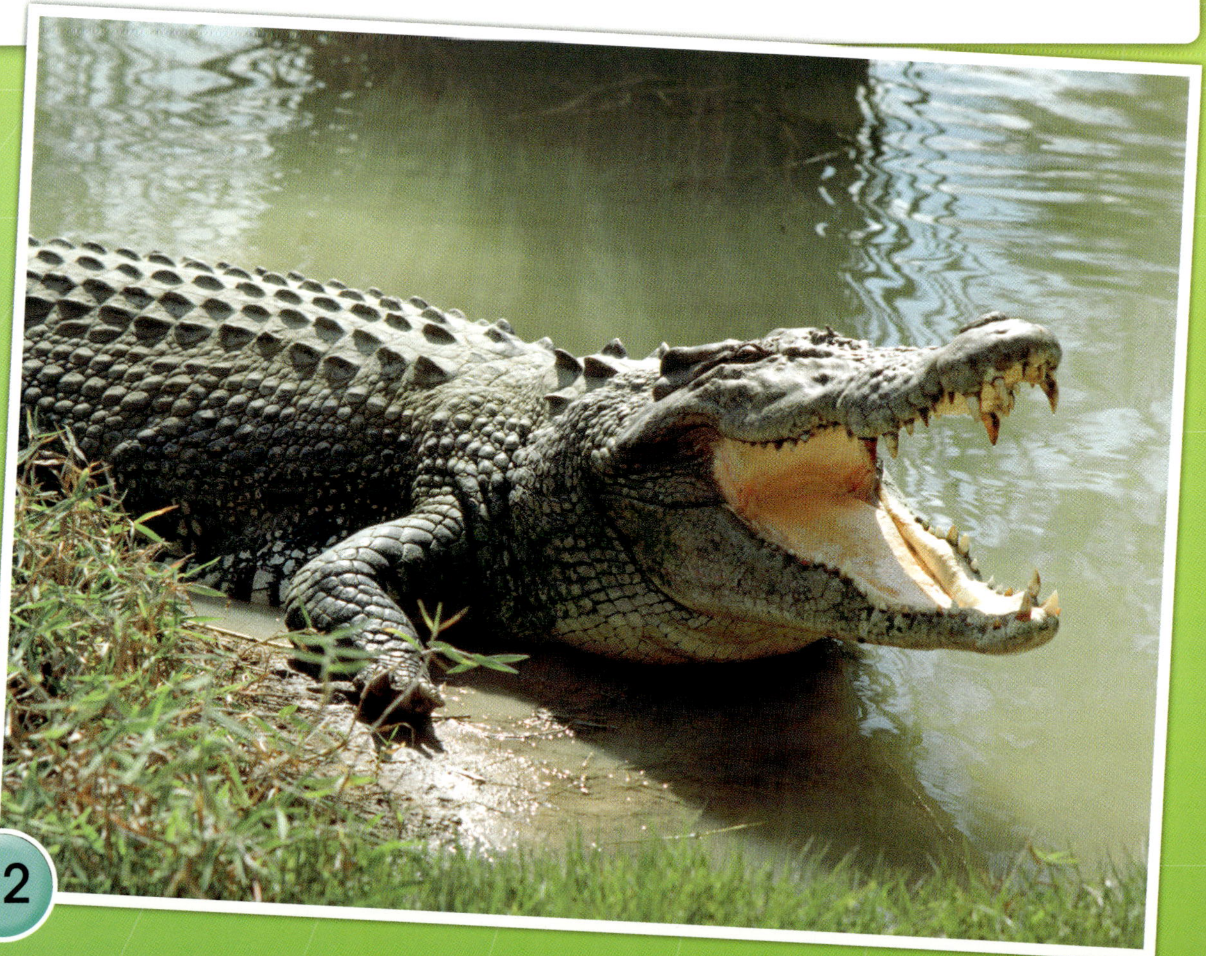

BARKO'S BLOG-TASTIC RIVER FACTS

Piranhas are small fish from South America. They are famous for their razor-sharp teeth. Some are fierce meat-eaters, but some only eat fruit and seeds that fall into the water.

Record-breaking river

Posted by: Ben Blog | 6 September at 6.13 p.m.

Next, we headed to Egypt to visit my favourite river – the Nile. It is 6,695 kilometres (4,160 miles) long – the longest river in the world. The ancient Egyptians used to live on the banks of the Nile. You can still see their temples and pyramids when you're taking a relaxing **felucca** ride.

felucca

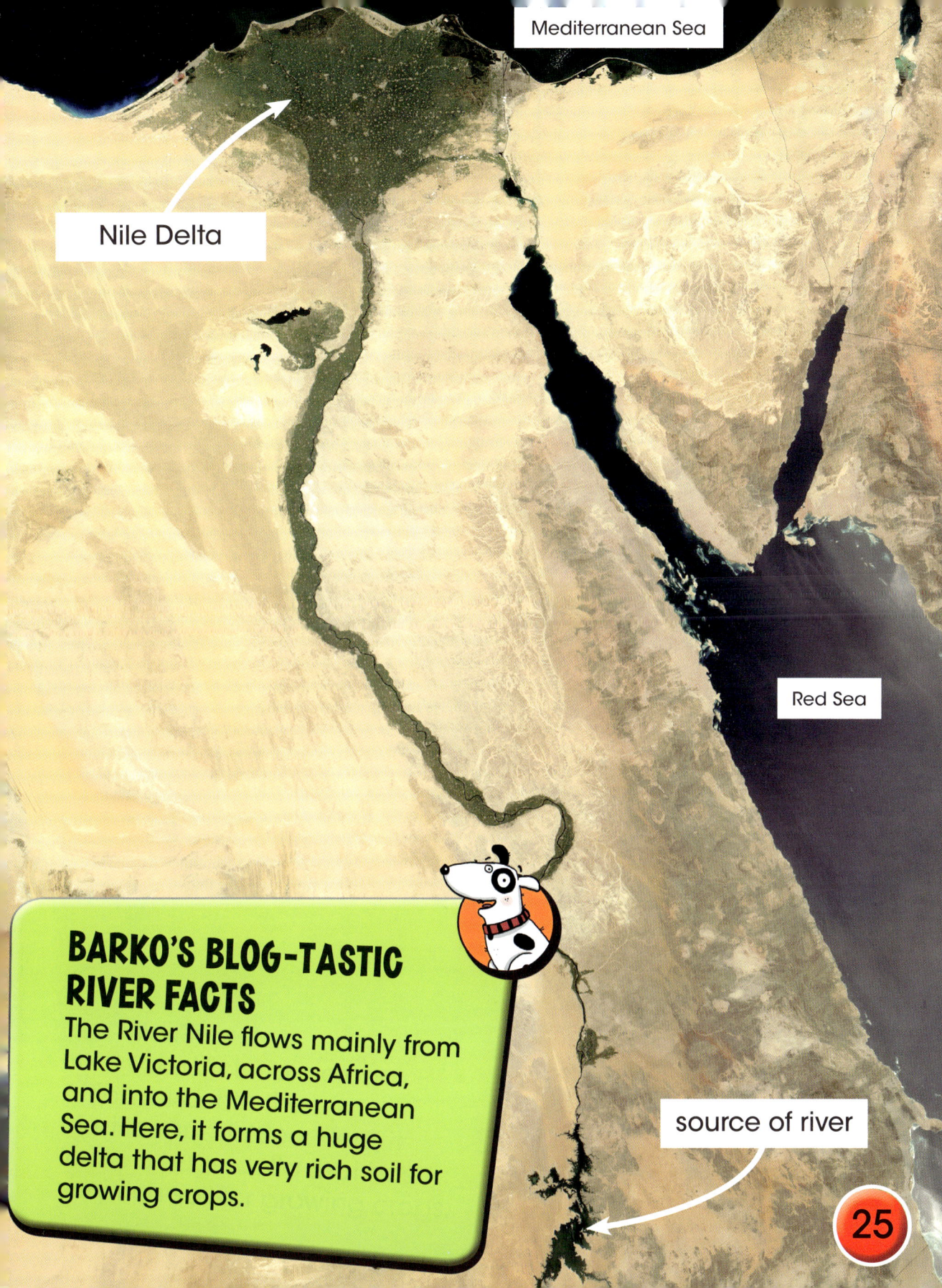

Mediterranean Sea

Nile Delta

Red Sea

BARKO'S BLOG-TASTIC RIVER FACTS

The River Nile flows mainly from Lake Victoria, across Africa, and into the Mediterranean Sea. Here, it forms a huge delta that has very rich soil for growing crops.

source of river

25

Ruined rivers

Posted by: Ben Blog | 13 October at 1.56 p.m.

Last stop on our trip was the River Rhine in Germany. For centuries, this river has been used for transport, and many factories were built on its banks. But it has also been used as a dumping ground for rubbish, chemicals, and **sewage**. Luckily, the clean-up has begun.

BARKO'S BLOG-TASTIC RIVER FACTS

The Yangtze river dolphin became **extinct** in 2006. It was only found in a few rivers in China, including the Yangtze River, one of the busiest and dirtiest rivers in the world.

Rushing rivers explorer quiz

If you are planning your own river expedition, you need to be prepared. Find out how much you know about rushing rivers with our quick quiz.

1. Where does the River Nile start?
a) Lake Nasser
b) Lake Victoria
c) Lake Superior

2. Which is the tallest waterfall?
a) Niagara
b) Victoria
c) Angel

3. What is a **meander**?
a) bend in a river
b) small river
c) river plant

4. Where does the Okavango River end?
a) in the sea
b) in the desert
c) in the mountains

5. What do piranhas eat?
a) meat
b) fruit
c) seeds

6. Which is the longest river?
a) Nile
b) Amazon
c) Yangtze

7. What is this?

8. What is this?

Glossary

canyon long, deep cut in Earth's surface

delta fan-shaped piece of new land that builds up where a river flows into the sea

extinct animal or plant that has died out forever

felucca sailing boat on the River Nile

glacier huge river of ice that flows down a mountainside

inquisitive interested in learning about the world

Marco Polo explorer who lived from about 1254 to 1324. He travelled from Italy to China.

meander huge bend or loop in a river

plain large, flat stretch of land

prey animals that are hunted and eaten by other animals

sewage waste from humans and animals

source place where a river begins

spring water that flows up from underground

streamlined smooth, tube-shaped. An otter's body is streamlined to allow easy movement through water.

tributary smaller stream that flows into a main river

Find out more

Books

100 Things You Should Know about Extreme Earth, Belinda Gallagher (Miles Kelly, 2009)

Harsh Habitats (Extreme Nature), Anita Ganeri (Raintree, 2013)

The Nile River (Read Me!: Explorer Tales), Claire Throp (Raintree, 2012)

The World's Most Amazing Rivers, Anita Ganeri (Raintree, 2009)

Websites

environment.nationalgeographic.com/ environment/habitats
This National Geographic website covers a range of habitats.

www.bbc.co.uk/bitesize/ks2/science/living_ things/plant_animal_habitats/read/1
Learn about habitats on this BBC website.

Index